The Remarkable Chameleon

The Remarkable Chameleon

Story and Photographs by Lilo Hess

Charles Scribner's Sons
New York

The Remarkable Chameleon

One of the oddest reptiles we know today is the true chameleon. When one looks closely at this little lizard, it reminds one of the long past age of dinosaurs. But dinosaurs, distant cousins of the chameleons, disappeared millions of years ago because they were unable to adapt to the changes of the earth. The chameleon, however, was able to change and develop a shape and a way of life so it could survive. All the remarkable features of this little lizard are specialized and highly successful adaptations for its life in the trees.

Chameleons have become world famous for their ability to change color, yet this is much exaggerated and one of their least significant features.

Chameleons are so different from other lizards that scientists have put them into a group by themselves. About eighty different kinds of chameleons are known, and they live in almost all parts of Africa and Madagascar. Some occur in India, Asia, and Ceylon, and one species is found in southern Spain.

Some live in the high altitudes of the mountains or in rain forests; others live in dry regions. They can be found in vineyards or on garden hedges, in bushes and in trees. Some are about three feet long, while others are only an inch and a half in length. The majority of them are between three and eight inches long.

The name chameleon comes from the Greek word *chamai,* meaning "on the ground," and *leon,* meaning "lion." Indeed, when the little creature stalks its prey, one is reminded of a lion, but why the Greeks used the word *chamai* is not known, since only one species lives on the ground—the rarely seen leaf chameleon.

Each species of this lizard has different ornaments. Some have long horns; some have short ones; some have helmets and hoods, while others are adorned with skinflaps, bony plates, sharp spines, prolonged snouts, or rounded shields.

No wonder such an odd-looking creature, which could also assume weird poses, was believed to have many super-natural powers. One folksaying advises: "Roast the left foot of a chameleon together with the plant of the same name, in

an oven, then mix with salves in a wooden container and the owner of this mixture will be invisible." Or "Put the right foreleg of a chameleon into a hyena skin and wear this on your left arm. This protects against robbery and assault." Another superstition: "Mix the head, throat, and liver of a chameleon with hard wood and burn it. This mixture is guaranteed to bring rain and thunderstorms." Folklore also warns children never to kill a chameleon since it might be one of their ancestors.

The first detailed description of a chameleon was given by Aristotle. He compared the changing colors of the chameleon to the changing moods of man. We still use this comparison today—"changeable as a chameleon."

In the Western Hemisphere another little lizard that can also change colors has been called a chameleon, though it is not related to the true chameleon of the Old World. Its real name is Anolis *carolinensis,* or just Anole. It is a slender, alert lizard often sold in pet stores, at country fairs or circuses. It lives in the southern United States and feeds on various insects, which it catches by running after them and grabbing them with its mouth. Its skin can change from various shades of brown to different greens; it may also be pale yellow or mottled. When it is caught by the tail, the tail may break off. In time the Anole will grow a new one.

The tail of the true chameleon does not break off, and if through an accident this does happen, it will not grow back again. It is prehensile, which means the chameleon can hang by it and use it to grasp twigs. When the tail is not in use, it is neatly curled up like the coil of a watch spring.

To climb trees, walk along thin, swaying branches or tops of bushes, the chameleon has to have an exceptionally firm hold. It is almost impossible to shake a chameleon out of a tree because of its specialized grasping toes.

Most other lizards have five long, slender toes on each foot. Ground-dwelling species have stout nails; climbing liz-

ards are equipped with sharp claws so that they can hook into tiny cracks in a wall or in tree bark. Some have adhesive pads and broad flat toes to help them cling.

The chameleon has no visible foot. The toes seem to sprout right out of the ankle and look like the grasping jaws of a pair of pliers. The toes are divided into opposing bundles. On the front legs there are three toes on the inside and two on the outer side. On the hind legs the toes are exactly reversed: three on the outside and two facing inward. The digits of each bundle are grown together except for the last joint, which terminates in a sharp nail. The chameleon can use its toes to scratch itself, remove a bad-tasting insect or a piece of dirt from its mouth, as well as to grasp twigs.

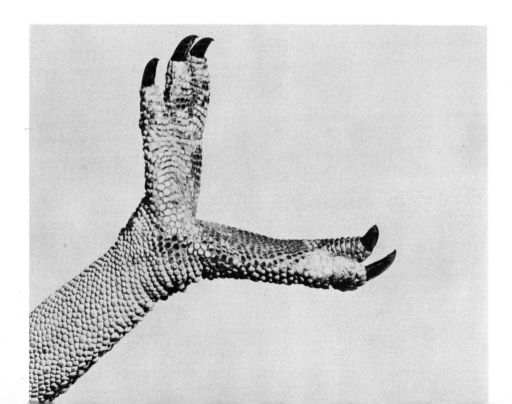

The legs are very muscular and thin, growing downward. The chameleon walks slowly and gracefully among the branches, placing one leg carefully in front of the other and lifting a leg only when it has found firm hold with the other. On the ground the chameleon shuffles along awkwardly.

A chameleon may sit quietly on the same branch for several hours. When it sleeps its closed eyes do not appear different from those of other sleeping lizards. But when it is awake, a strange staring eye bulges out on each side of the head. The skin of the eyelid encircles the entire eye, leaving only a peephole opening for the pupil. It is astonishing to see the eye swivel around in a complete circle. The eye is almost always in motion, looking up and down and to all sides. Since

each eye can move independently, the chameleon can watch front and back at the same time. Its vision is so keen that it can see the smallest fly walking between leaves several feet away.

The chameleon's hearing seems to be poor. There is no external ear opening and it probably feels vibrations the way snakes do.

Through the ages people have had weird ideas about the feeding habits of the chameleon. In early Christian times it was said that the chameleon sits with its mouth open so the wind can nourish it. The poet Shelley wrote: "Chameleons feed on light and air," and Shakespeare's Hamlet also speaks of the "chameleon's dish" being air. Now many people seem to believe that honey water is the right food for a chameleon. These strange beliefs might have come about because chame-

leons that get the wrong food or none at all in captivity will live for a few weeks before they starve. A healthy chameleon eats large quantities of various kinds of insects, and the giant three-foot-long chameleon is reported to eat small birds and mice as well.

A chameleon catching its prey is an amazing sight. When it spots an insect, the chameleon focuses both eyes on it with an almost hypnotic stare. Then the strange tongue flicks out with such lightning speed that the human eye can hardly follow the motion. Since the tongue always hits its mark, the eye nerves must be able to convey the distance and size of the victim to the chameleon's brain. The tongue can be extended more than twice the length of the chameleon's body. For long strikes the tongue is usually straight and may be curved for short ones. The top of the tongue is club shaped and covered with sticky mucus. This adhesive substance can hold even the most vigorously struggling insect until the tongue snaps back and the meal is chewed with the lizard's small teeth. When the tongue is not in use, it rests, pleated like an accordion, over a smooth, tapered, muscular stalk called the hyoid horn. The action of various muscles and the hyoid horn causes the tongue to shoot out to the desired distance and draws it back again.

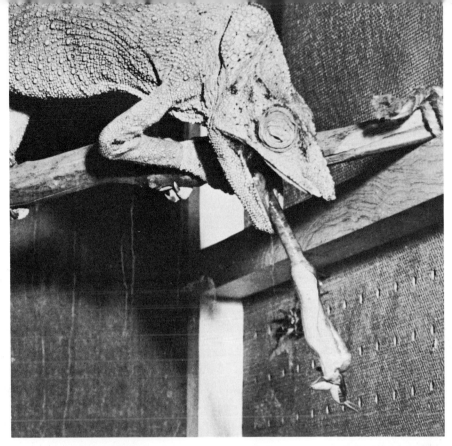

The skin of the chameleon is covered with granular and knobby scales. About once every few months the skin is shed. Unlike the snake, which can slither out of its entire skin like taking off a glove, the chameleon sheds its skin in bits and pieces. It helps the loosening of its skin along by rubbing against branches and pulling at the pieces with its grasping toes. It often eats its skin.

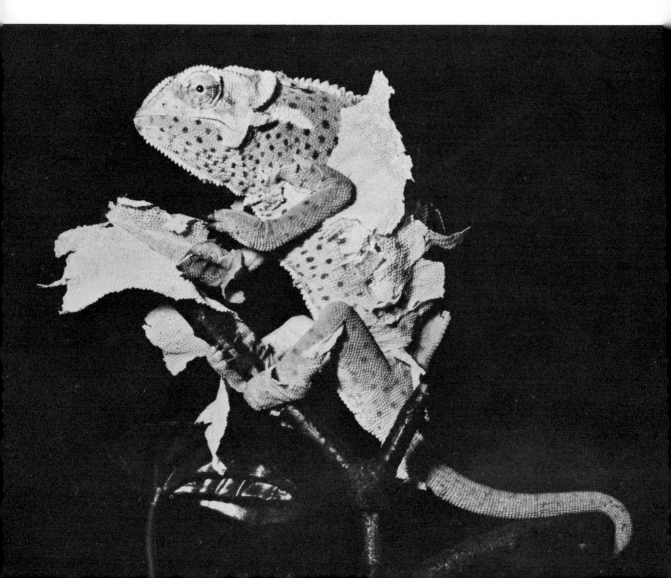

Almost everybody has heard the story that a chameleon can change colors to match its background. This is not so. Chameleons do change colors and can produce many different hues and patterns, but it is only a coincidence if its color matches the background. Each species is limited to its own range of color changes. A chameleon's color may be brown, gray, green, yellow, reddish, mottled, or spotted, no matter where it sits. The story that a chameleon on a plaid background was driven crazy because it could not decide to which color to change is just that— a story.

A chameleon changes colors as a result of its mood, the temperature, or light conditions. Some varieties can produce more color than others. Most chameleons have brown or green as their main body color. When they are asleep many fade into a ghostly off-white, while others turn pale yellow or light green. When they are excited they break out in spots or patches. When they are cold their color is lighter than when they are warm. But identical conditions will not always produce the same color or pattern in two chameleons sitting together: one might be dark brown and the other one green.

The chameleon's skin has several layers. Different color pigment cells are present in each layer. The inner layer has black pigment cells. Nerves control the expansion and contraction of the color cells. When the black cells rise and fall toward the skin surface, they blend, intensify, or blot out some of the other cells, thus making the different shades.

Since light influences the nerves that control the color cells, an interesting experiment can be made with most chameleons. A piece of cardboard, a paper lace doily, a pencil, or any other small object can be placed close to a chameleon

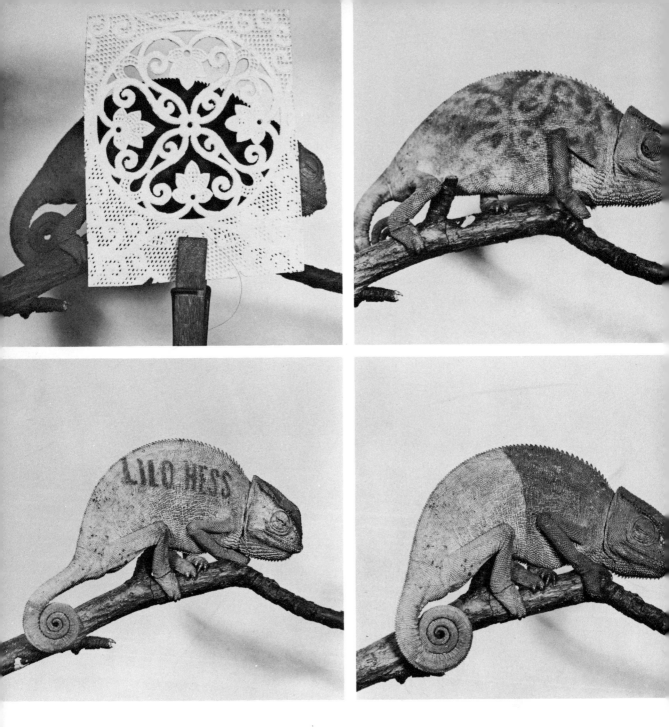

that sits quietly in one spot. If the chameleon is then exposed to a bright light from an electric light bulb or to strong sunlight for a few minutes, the shape of the object will show up clearly on the skin of the lizard. It will usually be a much lighter shade than the rest of the animal's body color. The pattern starts to fade almost as soon as the light is removed. By making cut-out letters in a piece of cardboard, one can produce legible words on the skin of the chameleon.

In many but not all chameleons the sexes can be distinguished by the absence or modifications of the head ornaments in the females. The strange horns that some chameleons display are never shed and never change color. They are comparable to the horns in cows. It is not quite certain if the males use the horns in real fights, but some are reported to push each other off the branches with their horns or elongated snouts.

All chameleons are quarrelsome. They puff, hiss and put on a good show of fierceness when they meet other chame-

leons. The large chameleon *melleri* threatens an enemy by inflating its throat, showing its teeth, hissing and swaying from side to side. It makes jerky forward movements, as if striking, with erected side flaps. But it always retreats before actual contact with the enemy.

Chameleons are solitary creatures and seem to prefer to sit alone in a favorite place. Only during the mating season do the males search for the females. The male High-casqued chameleon crawls about restlessly until he finds a suitable female. Then he approaches her, rapidly swaying from side to side. Their body color darkens. At first the female fends off the male's attention by hissing. Her color becomes so dark it looks deep purple. The male crouches low in front of her, still swaying. When she is ready to mate, her color changes back to a mottled greenish brown. Mating takes only seconds, and then the two scramble away, probably never to meet again.

Most chameleons lay eggs, but some give birth to living young. The egglayers inhabit warmer regions, since they depend on the warm soil to incubate their eggs. The female makes a rare descent to the ground. After walking about to find a suitable spot, she digs a small hole with her hind legs. In it she deposits up to forty white oval eggs with sticky parchment-like shells. Then she covers the hole and walks

away, her job as a mother finished. The number of eggs laid may vary with the different species.

In colder regions the chameleon's eggs develop inside the female's body since the soil is not warm enough to incubate the eggs. The gestation period or pregnancy has been reported to be about four or five months. During this time the female becomes heavier, more sluggish, and does not change colors as readily.

A day before giving birth, the female walks restlessly up

and down the branches. Finally she selects a suitable branch, contracts her body, and the first baby emerges. It looks almost as if the female is laying an egg, since the baby is encased in a transparent sack of mucus. As the sack falls, it sometimes gets stuck to a leaf or twig, but the baby struggles so vigorously to free itself that it usually falls to the ground. As it hits the

ground, the membrane tears open and the baby is free. The intervals between the emerging babies seem to vary from one minute to about ten minutes. The last ones are slower to come, since the mother shows definite signs of exhaustion. Five to twenty-four babies might be born, depending upon the species.

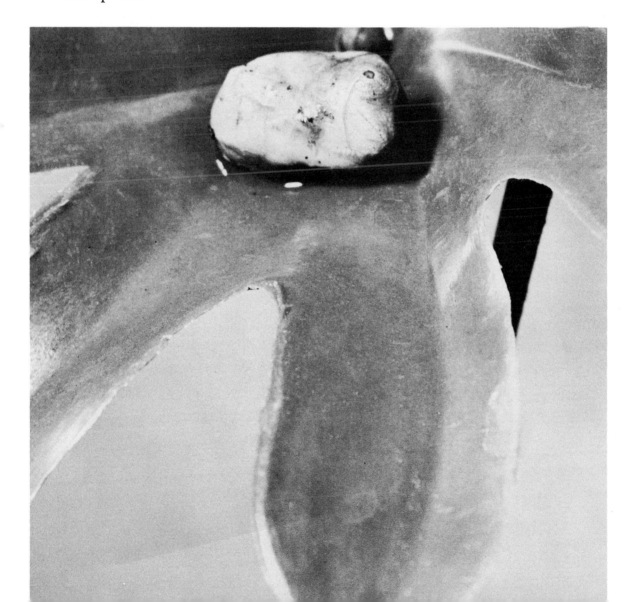

The new babies climb immediately up the nearest branch. Their legs are so thin and their toes so tiny it seems miraculous that they are so strong. The babies are miniatures of their parents, except for head ornaments, which develop later. The little tail is already prehensile, and if a baby loses its balance, the tail can hold it.

After all the babies have been born, the mother starts looking for food. If one of her babies is near, she might eat it. The babies also look for food immediately. The insects they eat have to be very small, like fruit flies, for instance. The babies can catch them just as quickly and accurately as their parents. They cannot make many color changes at this time and are mostly light or dark brown or have small spots and patches. They double in size in about two weeks. After that they grow more slowly.

"A seen chameleon is a dead chameleon" is an old folk-saying, and the babies as well as the adult chameleons instinctively stay well hidden to avoid detection. They have many enemies. Hawks, snakes, foxes and other lizards will eat them if they can find them. But the chameleon's color, skin pattern, and body shape blend so well with the background of sunlight and shadow of the foliage that they are extremely hard to see. The chameleon has still other ways to protect itself.

It can make its body so slim that it looks very much like a twig. If the enemy notices it, the lizard will turn its underside toward him, keeping the branch between them. No matter which way the enemy tries to attack, he will always have to bite into the twig first.

The chameleon can also pump its body full of air, enlarging it to a flat disk almost double its original size. The enemy might then find it too large to swallow. A slightly exaggerated sixteenth-century fairy tale tells of a hungry ser-

pent that wanted to eat a chameleon. The chameleon blew itself up into a large balloon, and to make itself still broader, it took a stick into its mouth crosswise. The serpent knew he could not swallow such a large morsel and went away hungry and discouraged.

Chameleons are often sold as pets, but they are extremely delicate and difficult to keep. They need the right kind of light, food, water, temperature, and a suitable container.

The best kind of container for the chameleon is a terrarium or a regular aquarium tank. The latter need not be waterproof. A six-to-eight-inch chameleon or several smaller ones can be kept in an eight-gallon tank. If an aquarium tank is used, a wire mesh top has to be put over it. The frame for the top can be made out of light wood or floor molding with mosquito wire stapled to it. The chameleon needs branches to climb on. It is best not to put soil into the bottom since the dirt might get stuck to the chameleon's tongue when it strikes at an insect on the bottom. There should not be too many twigs on the bottom because insects tend to hide behind them. Some leaves can be used to decorate the tank, but it is preferable to use plastic ones, which won't wilt.

The chameleon needs light and warmth. In the summer months the tank can be set outdoors in a partially shaded

place. In the winter the chameleon needs additional warmth. A 25-watt bulb in an aluminum reflector set above the tank will give off enough heat to keep the chameleon comfortable. Since most houses are warm during the daytime but have less heat at night, it is best to have the light bulb on during the night and place the tank in a warm spot during the day without the extra heatlamp.

Chameleons drink a lot of water, but they do not learn to drink out of a dish. In nature they lap up falling raindrops and dew from leaves and branches. In captivity one either has to sprinkle water frequently into the tank or let them drink out of an eyedropper. They learn this very quickly and open their mouths to drink the drops. Some chameleons seem to need water every day, while others drink only once a week. Newly purchased lizards might need water before they are able to eat. Some are so dehydrated that they are unable to catch their prey; their tongues do not seem sticky enough to hold the insects. They also frequently misjudge the striking distance. As soon as they drink water this condition is remedied.

Many chameleons will eat mealworms, which are easily obtained in pet stores. Tame chameleons will eat them from the hand, but a steady diet of mealworms is not good for them

and a change should be provided. Crickets are a satisfactory food and can be purchased in pet stores too. Some fish bait places sell live crickets. Large chameleons might consume fourteen to eighteen crickets daily; for them one can buy the crickets in quantities from "cricket ranches" at reasonable cost.

To store the crickets one needs a smooth, high-walled tub or tank so that they cannot jump out. It is best to get half-grown crickets, for they cannot jump as high as the large ones. Crickets can be fed bread, oatmeal, and sliced cucumber, lettuce or carrot for moisture.

The favorite food of all chameleons seems to be flies, but since it is a lot of work to catch enough flies for a good-sized chameleon, one might do what was done in former times in southern Spain. There, chameleons were sold in cages as living "flytraps." The chameleon in its cage was placed in a tree or other convenient spot, and a small piece of raw meat or fish was tied near it. The smell of the meat attracted the flies and the chameleon caught the flies. This works only if there are enough flies in the vicinity. The chameleon can also be put near an electric lamp outdoors on summer evenings so that it can catch the many small bugs and moths that are attracted to the light.

If several chameleons are to share the same home, they should be about the same size. If a small and a large chameleon are housed together, their owner might end up with just one large lizard.

Each chameleon has a distinct personality. Some are shy and easily frightened, while others are bold and aggressive; some like to be petted and handled, others panic when picked up, but they all quickly learn to know their keeper. It is fascinating to watch their strange ways and well worth the trouble it takes to care for these remarkable lizards.